HINDSIGHT
— it was just an afterthought —

ISBN 978-0-578-25531-6 (Paperback)

Any references to historical events, real people, or real places are used fictiously. Names, characters, and places are products of the author's imagination.

Front cover by A. L. Redden
Book design by A. L. Redden
Illustrations by A.L Redden

Printed by Lulu Publishing

First printing edition 2021

Lulu Publishing

www.brushandpendesignsco.etsy.com
Instagram: @a.l.redden.author

HINDSIGHT:
it was just an afterthought
By A. L. Redden

to the men I thought I loved,
thank you for the poems

&

to my family,
thank you for for believing in me
when no one else did
including myself

HINDSIGHT

An Introduction

Write something. I must write
something. Something that matters.
We all seek greatness somewhere.
To be remembered by generations,
to be looked at with respect.
A practical muse says *it is better to be feared than loved.*
My greedy heart wants both.
I choke on my need for greatness,
trip on my desire to make a difference,
fall on the urge to matter.
Drunk with the idea that if I work hard enough,
dream wild enough,
think loud enough,
they will know me.
I will be remembered.
But all this choking, tripping, falling
destroys any chance at being good.
Wouldn't it be better to be quiet,
humble, and live for others?
To grow fresh fruit,
to smile at strangers and invite
them in, to be kind
for their sake rather than my own ego?
There is this idea in my head:
why would anyone want
to read this, why
would I waste their
time, my breath, the earth's paper?
I stab myself in the back wanting fame and recognition.
And fail to do the simple and be good.

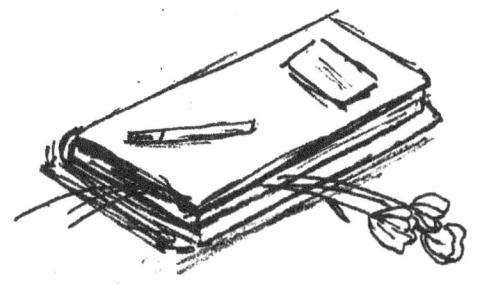

Car Ride

The sky is cloudy, the song says.
Trees rush past us,
snow in desperate clumps
hiding from the sun.
A deer, I say.
You nod,
silent jaw set. But I should have known

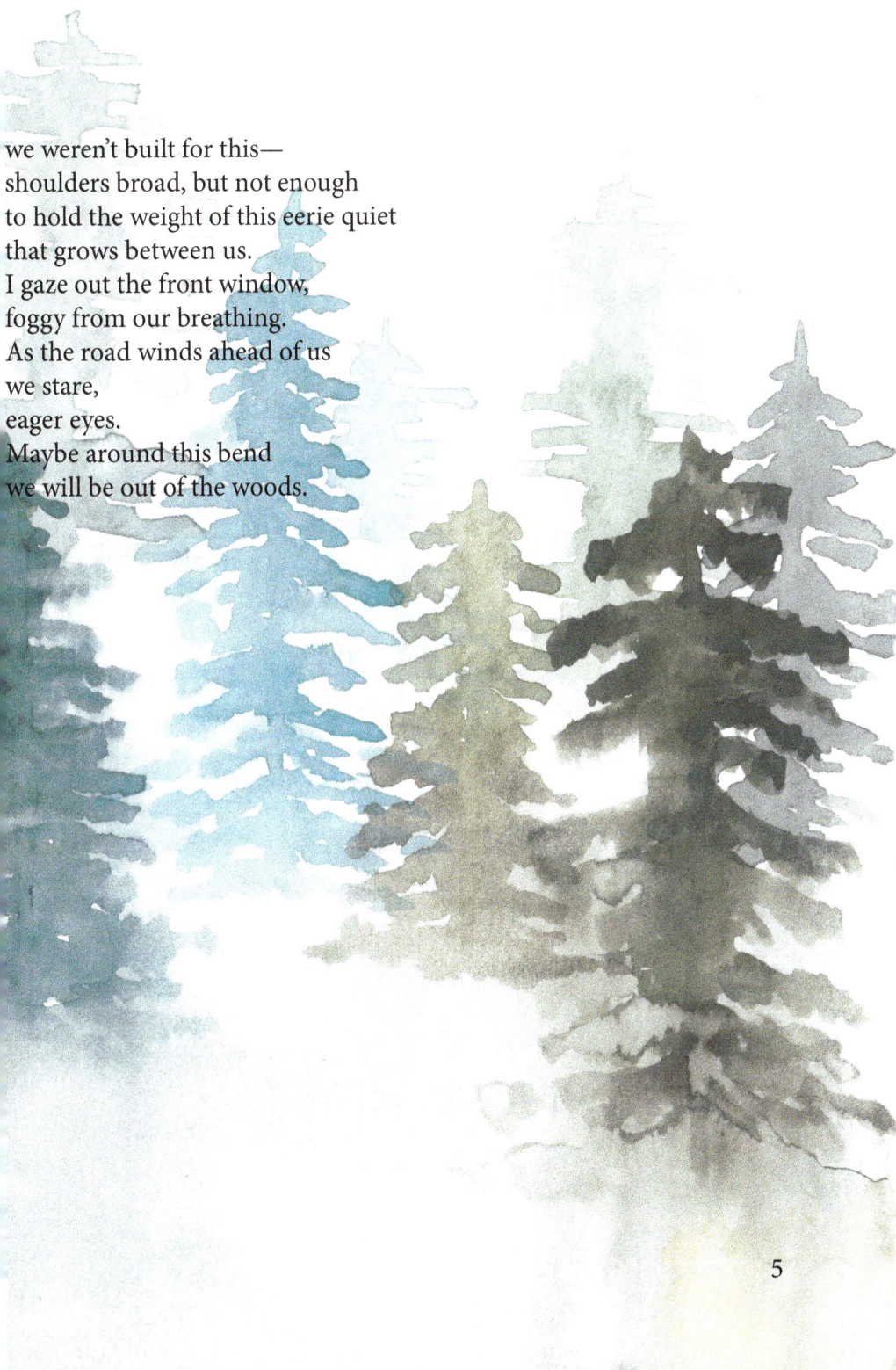

we weren't built for this—
shoulders broad, but not enough
to hold the weight of this eerie quiet
that grows between us.
I gaze out the front window,
foggy from our breathing.
As the road winds ahead of us
we stare,
eager eyes.
Maybe around this bend
we will be out of the woods.

City in January

The twisted streets ran across
callous skin. Towers grew up through the tough muscle and sinews,
like a child's elaborate model.
But still the grass poked its hair though the cracked sidewalks,
benches rested in the empty shade of domesticated trees,
and caged birds sang in the branches.
The garish loneliness of traffic stifled the small whispers
of a breeze that sputtered and died like the light of a fading streetlamp.
But high in the air
where the blue sky shone through the clouds
like shattered windowpanes,
flew the lucky, the few, the geese
that soared in smiles across the sky.
They landed in a park that's playing the part of the rebel,
pretending it is wild, exotic, and not from this neighborhood.
Like the young woman lying about her parents,
like the little boy dressed as an outlaw.
But they soon escaped when the air grew too cold and distant
and snow covered the iron spires that pierced the sky.
And night came early, turning the houses
into faces with a thousand gleaming eyes.

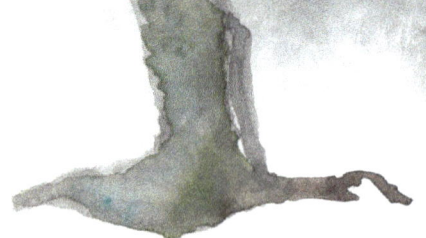

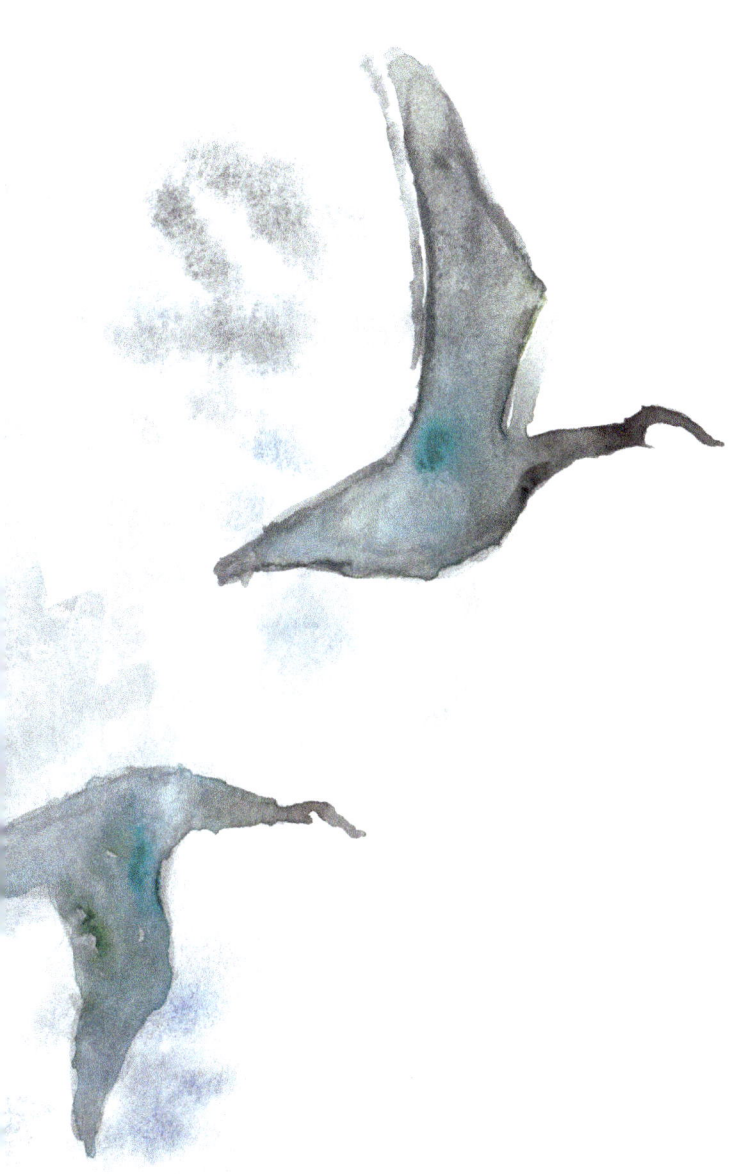

Mourning Mornings

The door was open,
the floor covered with books and clothes:
shells, armor from the day before.
9 in the morning.
Winter light was cold
even in the sun.
The smell of coffee from the kitchen,
the sound of paws on the carpet.
The morning light, illuminated the apples
of your cheeks.
Fuzzy hair and crinkled eyes.

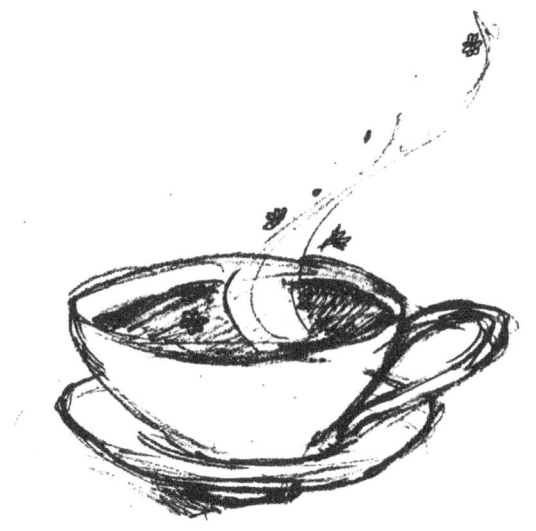

Somewhere between me coming into the room
and our eyes meeting

Somewhere between me saying hello
and you smiling

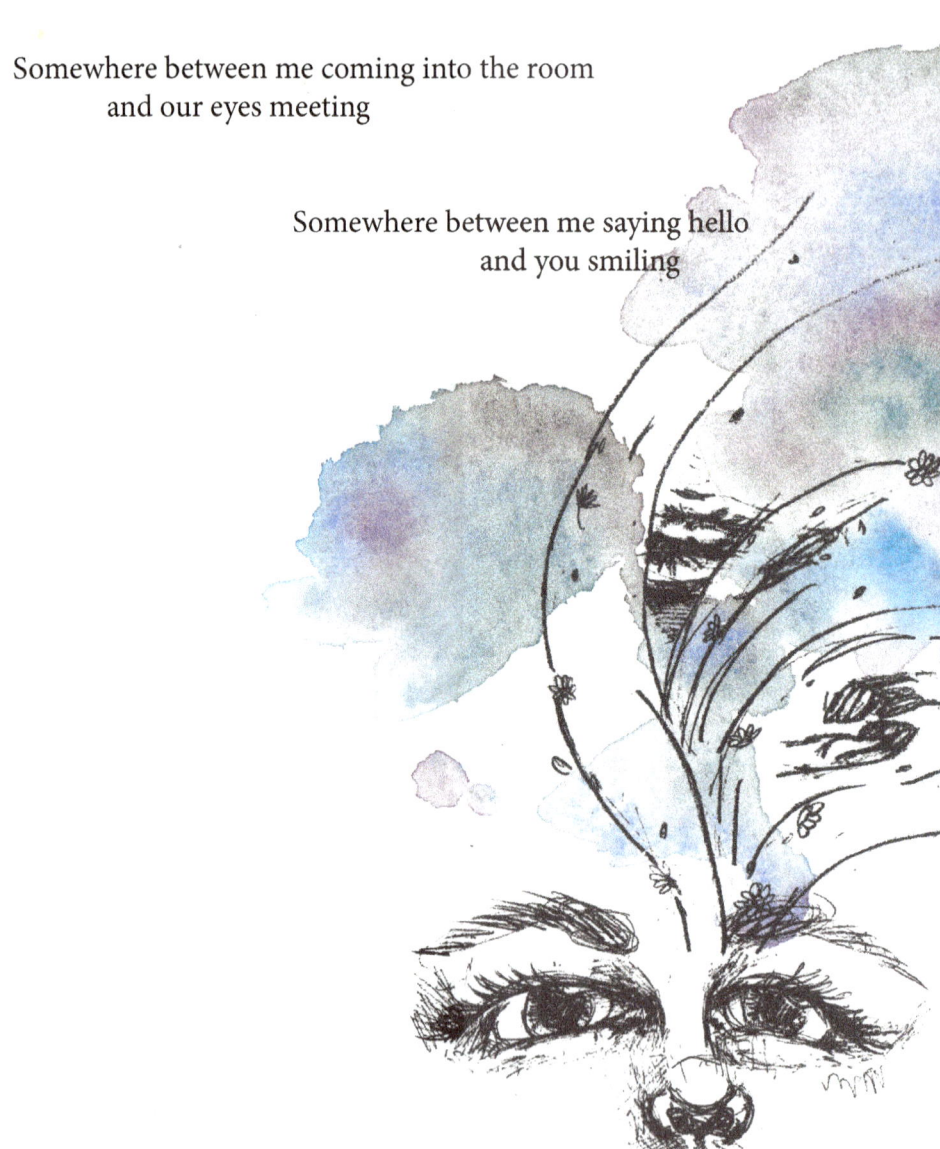

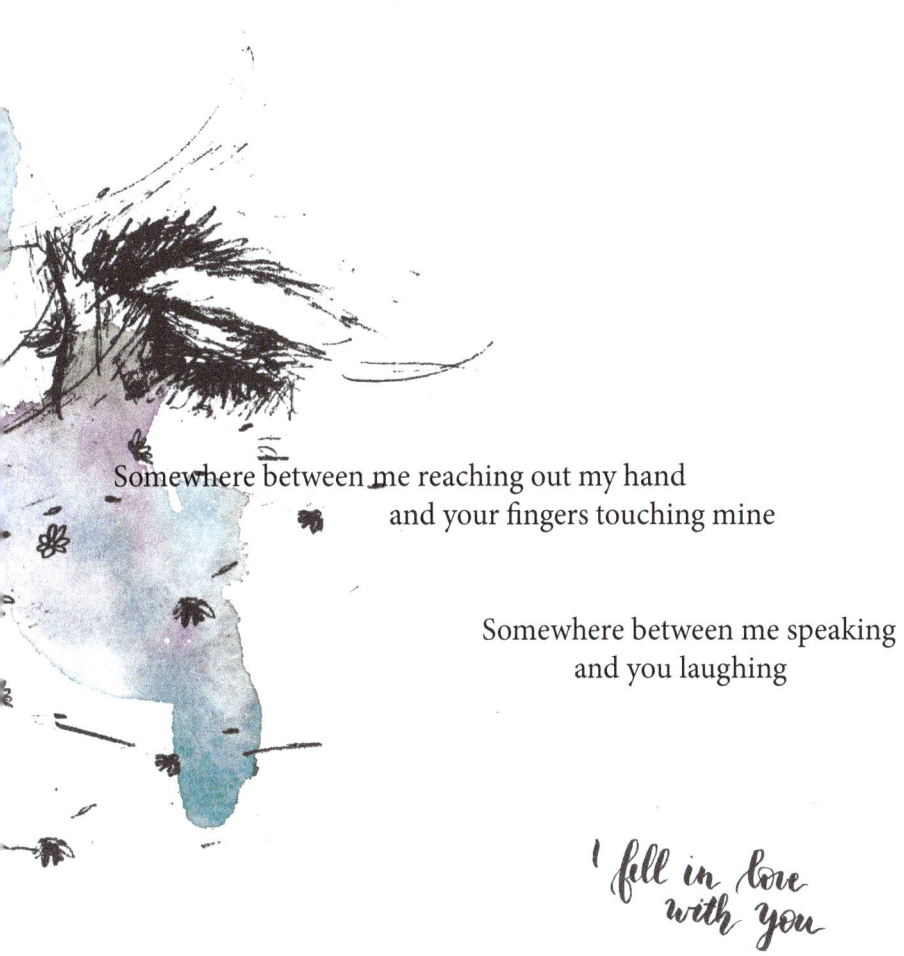

Somewhere between me reaching out my hand
and your fingers touching mine

Somewhere between me speaking
and you laughing

I fell in love
with you

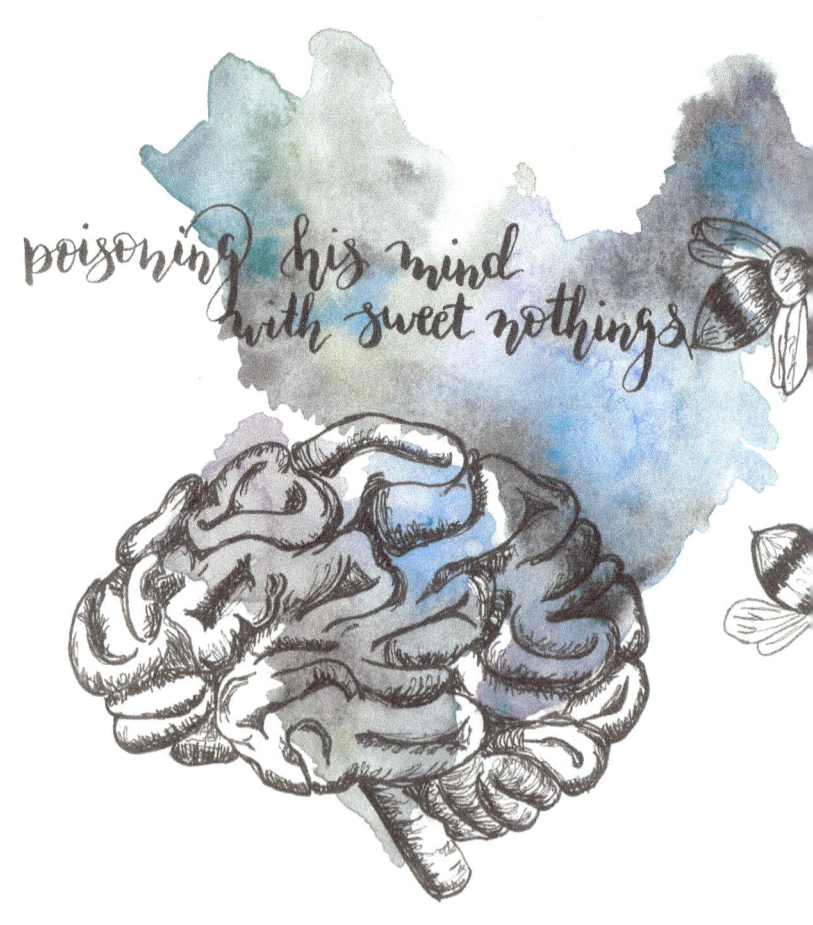

poisoning his mind
with sweet nothings

April Showers

It was early morning on a Saturday
and it had already started snowing.

The whole scene seemed like a dream
with the blossoms on the trees.

You were still asleep
on the mattress we called a bed

in the middle of our studio apartment. I climbed
back into the covers with a mug.

But even now with you tangled
in the sheets of our bed, I thought

of him. The way he smiled. The way he ran
his fingers through his hair.

The way he kicked the pebbles
down the cobblestone streets.

As I gazed at the snow falling to the ground, I knew
there would be no peaches this year.

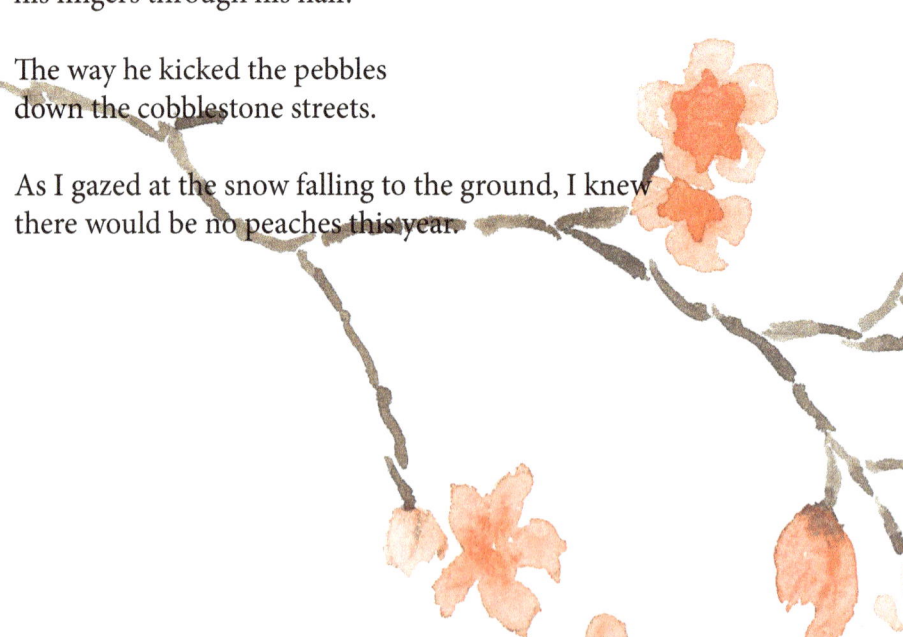

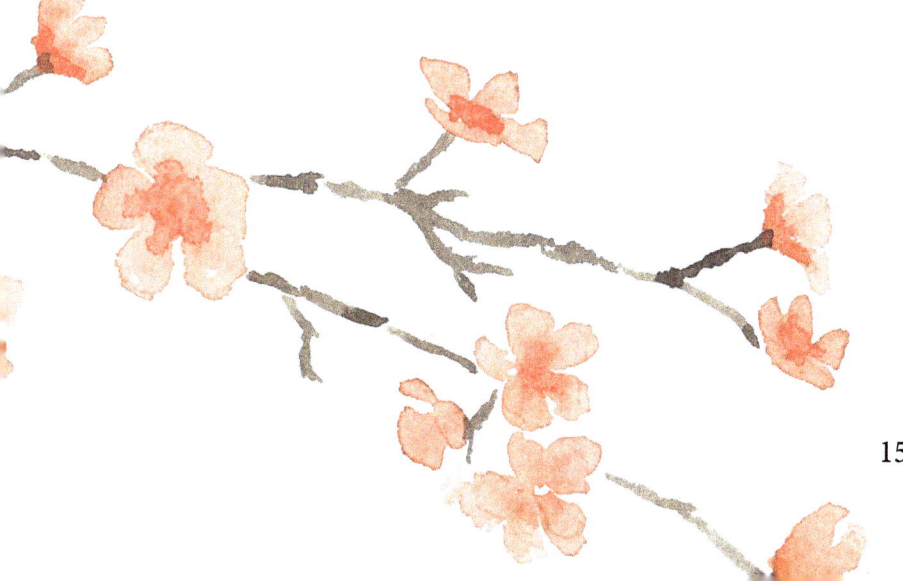

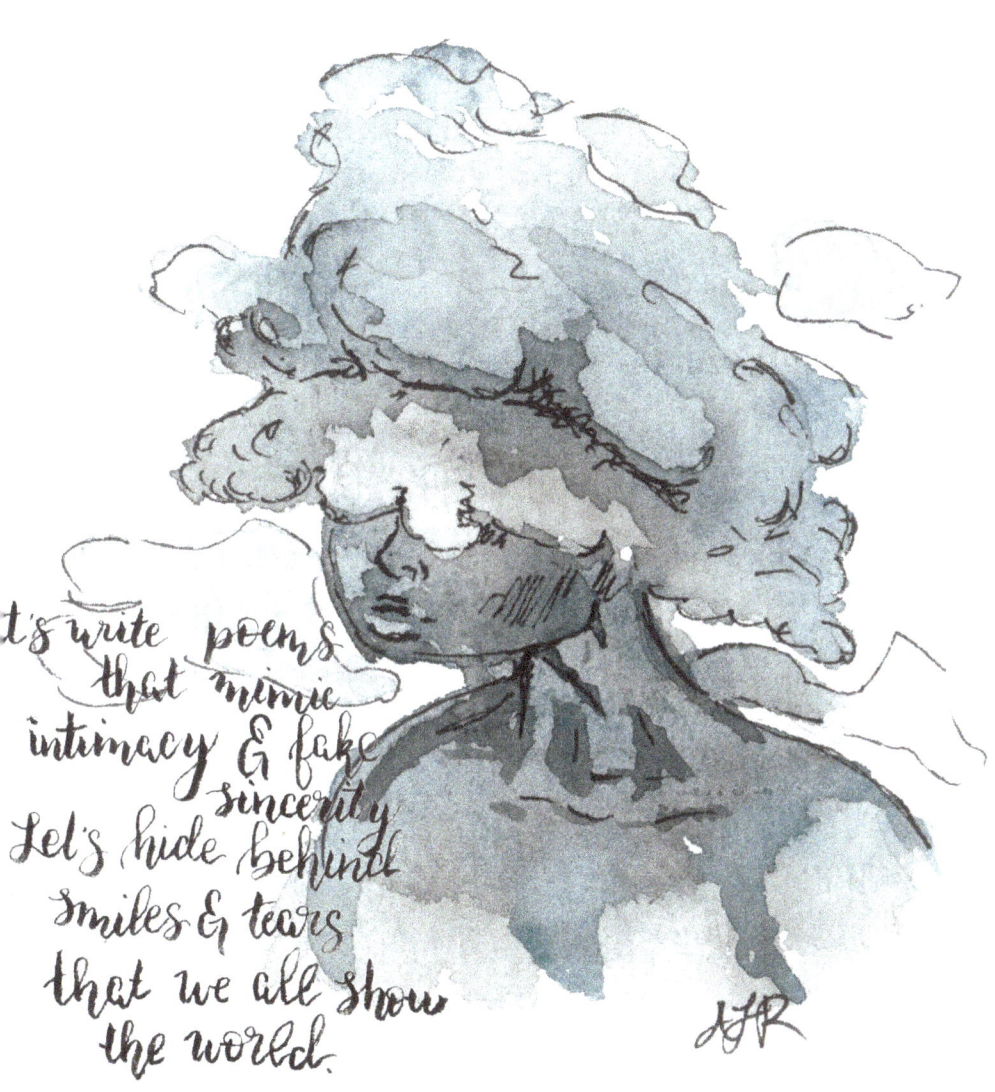

t's write poems
that mimic
intimacy & fake
sincerity
Let's hide behind
smiles & tears
that we all show
the world.

Books

People have always told me
Don't judge a book by its cover;
you don't know what they are going through.
But that isn't true.
You must look at their weathered, wind-beaten covers
to see the age in their faces. Look

at their scuffed and ruffed corners
for abusive scars. Their dog-eared pages
of memories that they cannot forget
and gashes and slashes from an irresponsible hand
that leaves them with wounds that mar
their once-pristine pages. Search for coffee stains

from late nights and early mornings. The writing in the margins
are the interpretations of their actions. Dusty jackets
and moth-eaten neglect, their past storms
cause mold to fester and gnaw. Weathered
and thin pages yellowed with age and the turning of the page
tell the stories of every reader in their greasy fingerprints.

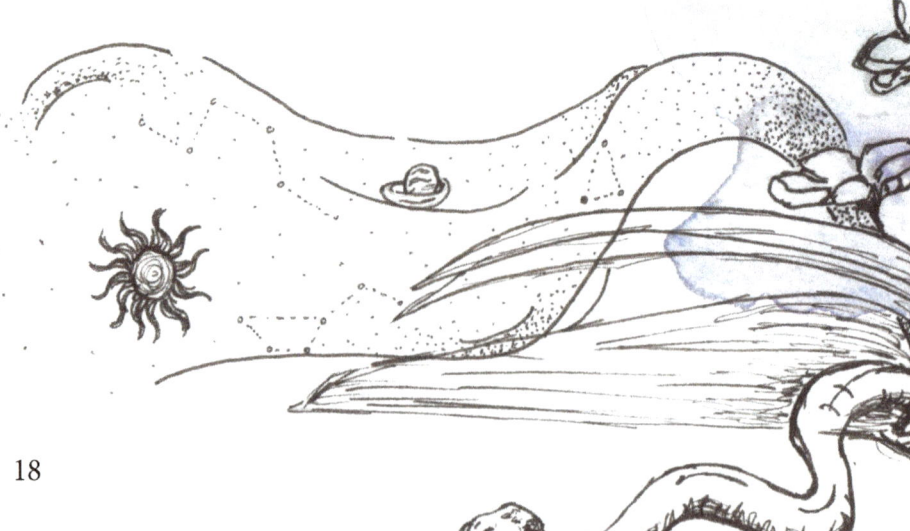

But most of all, look at their spine:
broken after years of abuse and reuse
without a tender and loving hand. Creases from force,
breaks from tragedies, buckling from carrying the weight
of all those who came before, stacked in precarious piles. We are the books
on the shelves of a library judged and searched

to find our lives hidden among the pages of time.

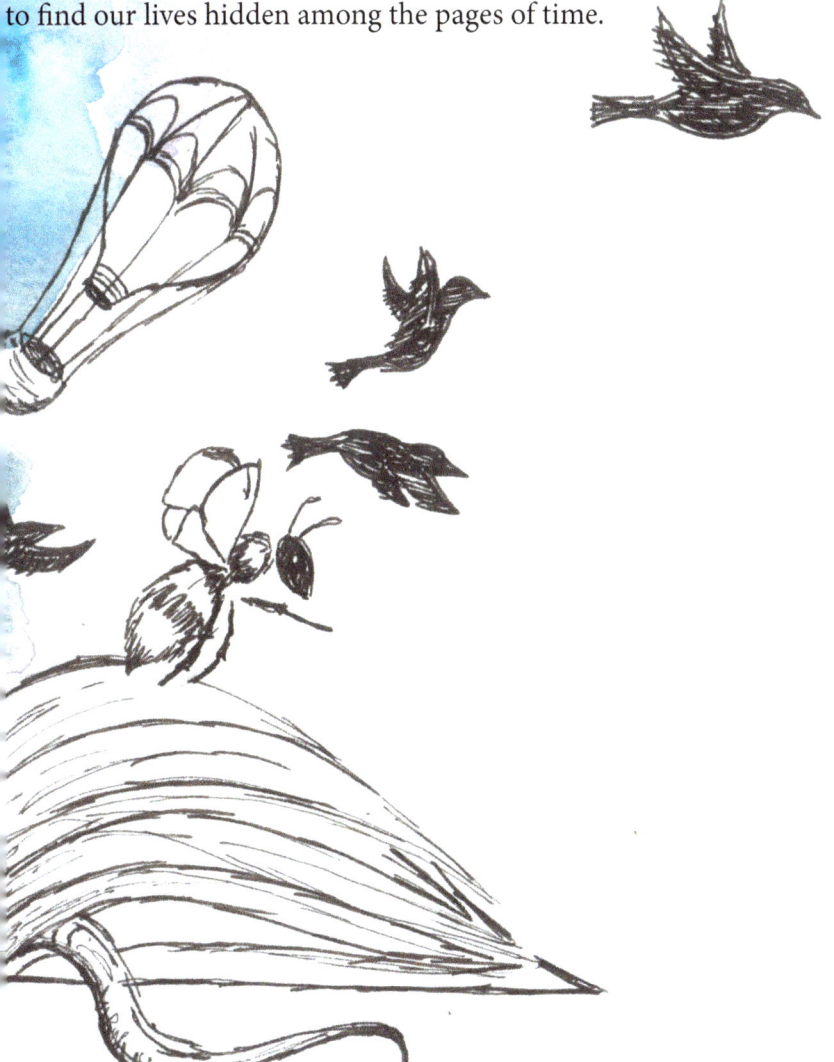

Keszthely

Running through the streets in the rain,
in the dark, soaked hair and clothes
dripping with laughter,
lungs bursting, cheeks aching,
still we ran. Behind us
the dimmed lights of cul-de-sacs
and before us the possibility of neon signs
that hung in shop windows
turning off as *Sorry, We're Closed* signs flipped
in store fronts on rough cobblestone streets. Wide smiles.
Flushed cheeks and crinkled eyes.
That is how I remember you:
alive,
young,
full of summer and cities,
taking me from the suburbs.

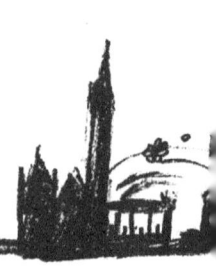

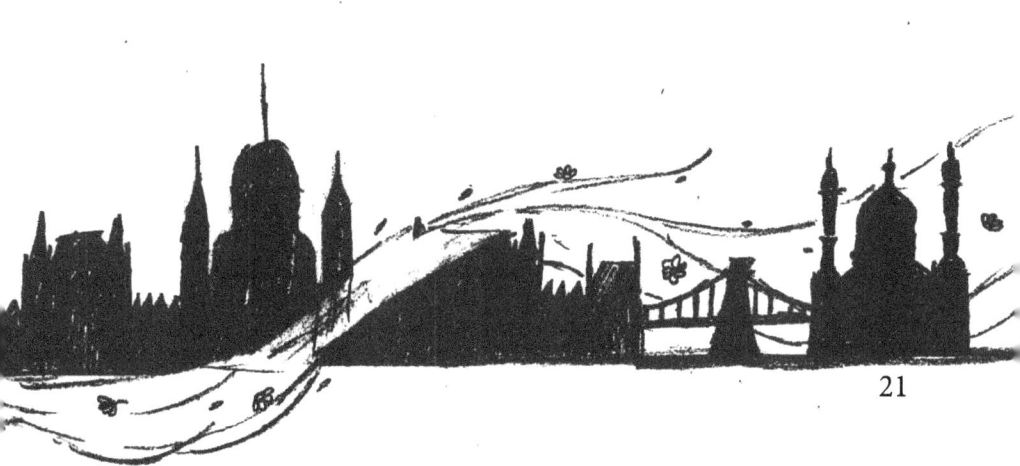

21

Unsent Letter

I opened the notebook and tried to write you something that would matter,
something that would echo down the halls of time to fall at your feet,
something that would make you smile,
something that would ring out over this city calling for people
to wake up and live.

But the pen ran out of ink
and the music wasn't right.
Instead I rambled about the weather and the news,
I spoke in wasted clichés that are still hungover from the night before
when I told you that your eyes were stars,
that you have a mind that could lead millions,
that your face shines like the sun.

Anyway, it is raining here and I need you
to light up this cloudy street.
Somewhere ahead, there is loud music
pumping from a car lulled at a stoplight,
murmurs from the people at this coffee shop,
whispers of ignorance and complacency. Enjoying
their yachts. Forgetting the tip, but remembering to drag
their eyes over the waitress.

If you were here,
there would be crowds around you, you
preaching, telling them about all the injustices, creating
your own little army of believers. Leading them into the fray, protesting
callousness, greed, and the devaluing of human life.
But I have always been quiet and too much of a dreamer to act,
too in love with the sound of pen on paper to sing the anthem of change.

Anyway, my coffee is getting cold,
and I am tired,
so I will finish this letter later
when the moment is right,
when I find new ways to start a revolution.
And to say

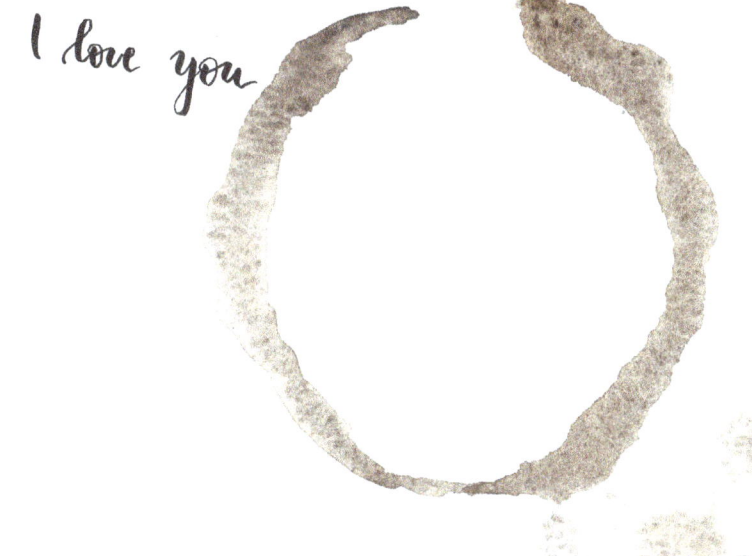

I love you

Hindsight

In the silences as you
watch the news I can hear your body aching:
Somewhere there is an alternate universe where none of this has happened.

Where the sun is shining
and you are complaining about long lines
and seeing that relative who chews loudly at the table,
who listens to talk radio, only to regurgitate it at dinner.
A time when you are wishing you were home more
and your biggest annoyance is that your coffee has gone cold
before you could drink it,
and you have to go out and walk the dog.
How I wish we could go back to those sweet annoyances,
those comforting irritations,
instead of this invisible monster eating our freedom, dreams, and lives.

Oh, that we could go back to the past
and repeat it,
but not that rosy one.
No, not the one filled with golden light like an old photograph,
but the one filled with overcrowded subway cars and bars
and chatty students who complain about tests:
those troublesome normalcies that filled your mind.

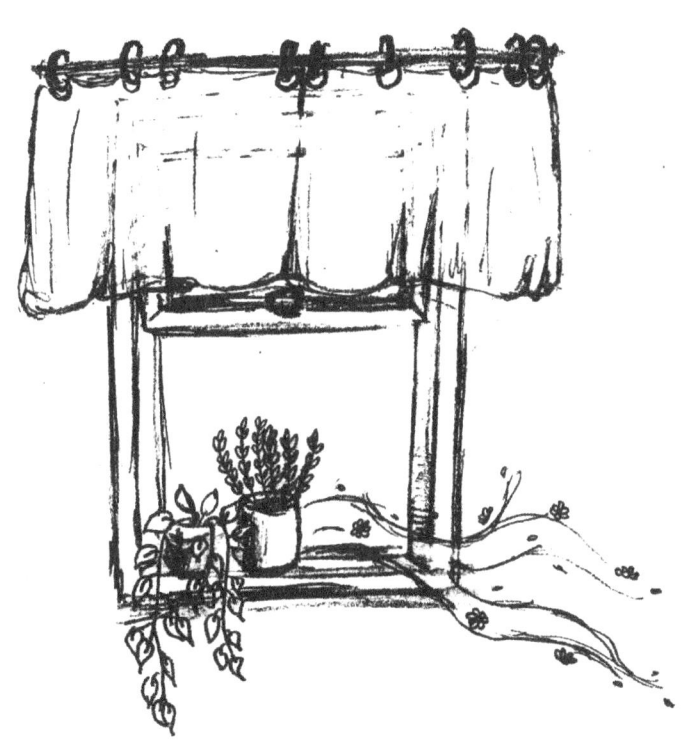

don't go to sleep

       yet

yet

yet

push the fog from your brain

keep your eyes from fading

feel your heart beating

       tick   tick   tick

                      tick   tick

slower   slower   slower

                           stop

Acknowledgements

There were many magical places in my childhood home: a cubby under the stairs, the gabled roofs of the top floor, the steep gully in the woods. But there was hardly a place that was more pure magic for such a small, concentrated point in time than the bunk beds shared with my siblings. We hung blankets like walls and a lantern from the slats of the top bunk, and we imagined it was the lower deck of a ship. But the real magic was the books my older sister would read to us. There my love of reading, and in turn writing, began.

There are so many people that I could mention who helped me start this project, but here are just a few. Thank you, Tell Tell editors who looked at my work and gave me the encouragement I needed to see my work was worth something. I'd also like to thank Heather Laurence, Amber Shrag, Lauren Jones, and Leah Rienhart who encouraged me to start and continue this project. Thank you to my wonderful parents, John and Claudia Redden, to whom I dedicate this book. There are not enough words in the English language to describe my thankfulness to them for their undying love and support. I'd also like to thank my siblings, Bethany Redden, Andrew Redden, and Jennine Redden for their love and laughter; thank you for making me who I am today. Lastly, and most importantly, I'd like to thank my Lord, Jesus Christ. He is Creator and the only reason I can create something as small as this chapbook. I pray that I can give Him glory through my craft.

I'd also like to thank you, dear reader, for picking up this collection and reading my poems. I hope they meant to you even a fraction of what they meant to me. I hope and pray that you stay curious, passionate, and creative. Keep reading!

www.ingramcontent.com/pod-product-compliance
Lightning Source LLC
Chambersburg PA
CBHW061234180526
45170CB00003B/1293